For Henry —
Gratitude,
Solitude

DRUG AND DISEASE FREE

Michael Broder

M. Broder

Also by Michael Broder
This Life Now

DRUG AND DISEASE FREE

Michael Broder

Indolent Books

Editor: Jameson Fitzpatrick
Book design: kd diamond
Cover art: Nayland Blake

Published by Indolent Books,
an imprint of Indolent Enterprises, LLC

www.indolentbooks.com
Brooklyn, New York

ISBN: 978-1-945023-01-9

CONTENTS

FOREWORD

What does it mean to be free?

In this book, Michael Broder offers us several possibilities. Indeed, the very first poem in the collection concludes with a declaration of freedom, an absolution achieved through love:

> I blame you, and you are blamed, and there you lie,
> sleeping like an angel, guilty as the devil, and I love you and I am free.

The claim is as sincere as it is aware of its own implausibility: the poem's title, after all, is "Atonement," not "Absolution." Broder orders the list of miseries with a poignantly knowing humor characteristic of his work, moving from the small mistakes and inconveniences in which the speaker must play some part ("missing the subway," "stains that won't come out in the wash") to the grave and impossibly large, blaming the beloved "for every mother [he] ever disappointed, / every boyfriend who ever died" and "every disease anyone ever contracted anywhere in this world / or on worlds yet to be discovered or never to be discovered."

Disease, like freedom, is a central preoccupation of this collection—as the title *Drug And Disease Free* suggests. Written over a span of twenty years, these poems up-end the antiquated but still all-too-common abbreviation "ddf" (online shorthand for having neither an STI nor an interest in hard drugs) to reconsider what it might mean to be truly free of and from disease. In reverse chronological order, Broder documents the life of an HIV-positive man who survived the worst years of "purple lesions, thinning hair" and has found an abiding love in a serodiscordant relationship. "October 18, 1990," which begins with an epigraph by Broder's husband, the poet Jason Schneiderman, invokes the myth of Orpheus and Eurydice to dwell on this meaningful difference in status:

> you who risked looking back,
> took the chance you'd be the one
> to emerge from love's underworld alone.

But importantly, these poems demonstrate that the tensions in this relationship are, for the most the part, mundane as in any other ("I Married A Slob"), and eclipsed by the profound solace of romantic partnership. The cocktail of true love and antiretroviral drugs has, for the most part, freed the couple of the book's first section from the grip of fear, delivering them into a life of domestic bliss (and, occasionally, resentment).

The increasing length of the book's sections is revealing: only the past gets longer. "Mad about a Boy," is followed by "More Plague Years," a title which alludes not only to the many lives lost to HIV/AIDS, but also to the vast body of literature produced in response to the epidemic, and, finally, "Other Boys," which works its way back to the speaker's first time having anal sex in "Fall 1981."

"More Plague Years" mourns the loss of lovers and friends, including activist and Broder's fellow classicist Rand Snyder, to whom he dedicates the prose poem "Progressive Multifocal Leukoencephalopathy," as well as the speaker's own diagnosis ("Surprising thing: the response of lovers / was to make love to me—"). Released from a handsome lab tech's tourniquet and leaving his appointment in "At the Phlebotomist's," he once again declares, "I am free." The book's nearly-titular poem, "Drug and Disease Free Seeks Same for Safe, Sane Sex," tells the story of a woman who, through the technological advent of "sperm washing," bears the child of an HIV-positive man two years after his death. In Broder's verse, what is "safe" and "sane," indeed, what is "sex," cannot be reduced to a question of HIV status.

"Standing Before the Ark" lends yet another, more complicated perspective: the extent to which, during the "Plague Years," seroconverting might have itself been a form of freedom from the anxiety of uncertainty:

Do you want this scarlet letter, pink triangle?
To become what you will be?

This tag in my blood a kind of invitation, proposal, corsage.
Marked, branded, known associate—believed.

The function of sex in this book is paradoxical: in the age of HIV, at once a formal constraint and a mechanism by which men cruising in Central Park still might "[transcend] the bounds the gender, race and class"—or come as close as possible. The poems in "Other Boys" chart both the liberating joys of sex and the feelings of gay shame that prevailed when Broder was coming of age in the 1970s and 80s; in "Fall 1981," when the speaker fingers his first trick, it is "disgusting." The poem ends back at home, where his dog "sniffs" his now-washed "crotch" and he worries "my God, he knows."

My role as Broder's editor was simple: through the revision and reordering of these poems, which include the first he ever published, to allow him to tell us all he knows about freedom, disease, and the relationship between them as clearly and as generously as possible. The strength of these poems lies both in the immediacy of their language and original composition as well as in the clarifying power of hindsight.

Drug and Disease Free makes an important intervention in the canon of contemporary gay poetry, in which so much writing about HIV/AIDS has remained in the realm of elegy. Even as many of these poems find Broder grieving, he is not confined by his status or the pains he has suffered. Ultimately, the triumphant possibility he realizes in this book is that freedom can take innumerably more forms than previously believed. The example of Broder's poetry proves that even in the face of inconceivable loss, we are free to conceive of a world in which we can keep loving, writing and remembering.

Jameson Fitzpatrick
February 2016
Brooklyn, NY

Mad About a Boy

Atonement

Because it *is* about blame, and I blame you—
for missing the subway, getting there late, having a bad time.
I blame you because I have to blame someone:
I mean, how could I live in a world where bad things just happen,
a universe where things aren't either bad or good?
It's so nice having you to blame—
for stains that don't come out in the wash,
yogurt gone sour in the fridge. For a long time

I had only myself to blame—
for sharpened number 2 pencils left home,
bicycle tires gone flat, spelling tests failed,
having pimples, smelling bad. That was insuperable,

and it only got worse when the crimes became more egregious—
interviews botched, jobs lost, rent paid with huge
cash advances on my credit card.

Oh, I tried other solutions, casting blame in other directions—
Mom and Dad, brothers, sisters, friends, teachers,
the ex he went back to, him.

But it never worked, not well, not for long.
No, because they were never willing;
you see, that is the beauty of you—
how you swallow what is cast in your teeth.
You are so good at being blamed; you are the blame meister,
because you know you have done wrong,
know the wrong you have done, how much wrong,
and you know you have done it to me. I blame you—

for every mother I ever disappointed,
every boyfriend who ever died,
every crackhead who robbed my apartment,
every disease anyone ever contracted anywhere in this world
or on worlds yet to be discovered or never to be discovered.

Yes, of course, of course it had nothing to do with you—
you weren't even born yet half the time.
And yet, what has that to do with anything?
I blame you, and you are blamed, and there you lie,
sleeping like an angel, guilty as the devil, and I love you and I am free.

October 18, 1990

God loves an expiration date.
—*Jason Schneiderman*

Best when used
before date stamped on top,
sell-by date,
freshness date,
date of my diagnosis,
my spoilage.
I was better used before, safer.
But 10 years post-expiration,
you found me on a shelf,
intriguing, older
dating someone else.
You deemed me a safe emotional bet:
hypochondria would protect you,
you could never love a disease vector,
sustain such high risk.
But the heart doesn't work that way,
and we were each other's *bashert*,
the Jewish version of Zeus's scales,
tossed dice. Loving me, you had no choice
but to make good use of my infection.
You took it like a height to be defended,
built walls around it,
turrets, aimed your guns.
Back then you thought love would declaw you,
tenderness soften your edge,
or that you were Eurydice,
always disappearing
when a man looked at you over his shoulder.
But this time it was you who risked looking back,
took the chance you'd be the one
to emerge from love's underworld alone.

I Married a Slob

They pile up in hazardous profusion,
your tee shirts, tank tops, underwear and socks.
Our linens mix in riotous confusion
with gym bags, sweatpants, combination locks.
The laundry hamper blocks the closet door,
and though he won't admit it to the gloom,
the spider crawling on the parquet floor
beneath the bed has never seen a broom.
To Lefferts Boulevard, Far Rockaway,
the sunlight gleaming on its silvery back,
from subway darkness bursting into day
the A train clatters on its rumbling track.
I slip my key into the padlocked door;
love's whisper lulls the world's chaotic roar.

I can't blame you

for cheese left out on the counter
overnight, hat left on the subway seat
as I dashed from local to express.

Can't blame you, away in your manger,
nestled in some swaddling, doing your thing.

How unfair of you to leave me like this,
accountable to no one but myself,
left to my own devices—

We   know   where   THAT   leads.

When I visit you there, it is analgesia only,
not healing.

You must come back to me,
to the nest I feathered for you,
the blanket-lined cardboard box
where I dropped you by the scruff of your neck.

You must doff your charade of being anything at all without me.

You must come home, and be my due.

The Bed

I used to lie in the center,
arms clasped around two pillows,
body aslant, legs spread,
taking up my lion's share.
Now for months I've lain alongside you,
on one side of an imaginary line,
my pillows beside your pillows,
so that when no one is in the bed
but only a comforter piled in a heap,
anyone looking can still see—
here lie two.

The Rock

Was it mine before it was ours,
this rock we call our own,
where we perch with coffee and bagels weekend mornings?
I can't remember that far back, or what I did
before you and your powers of recollection.
I must have invented the past, yesterdays that had to be,
to suit the mood or provide a clue
to whatever happened next.
Today I sit here alone and ask myself if you exist
or if I only imagined you
without you here to tell me whether or not we ever met.

More Plague Years

Progressive Multifocal Leukoencephalopathy

For Rand Snyder (1960–1996)

You can't really I don't think write it today the kind of poem Sappho wrote six
hundred years before Christ where you surprise the world saying not an army
is it on horseback or of foot soldiers or a fleet of sailing ships that on the black
earth is the most beautiful thing but rather whatever someone loves because
no one I think would be surprised when the poet says the most beautiful thing
is what one loves rather that would be expected and in fact to call armies
beautiful would I think be surprising to the modern reader although of course
there are subtleties to all of this for example we do today still think ships are
beautiful although we tend to romanticize sailing ships ships from the past
ships that remind us of an earlier time or at least bring to mind what we think
an earlier time was like and we think that time was simpler and therefore
better than now.

Dealing

How did I accomplish so much on the very first day?
Told my best friend, my therapist, my doctor,
had blood drawn for a T-cell count,
joined a support group, went home and listened
to a metaphysical healing tape.

Days went by, I told other friends, ex-lovers,
the boardwalk trick I was currently fucking—
one of my early experiments in topping.

Surprising thing: the response of lovers
was to make love to me—
terrycloth bathrobe falls away, we tumble to the futon.
Never felt so loved in my life.

The doctor pulls out his Walter Reade staging chart,
tells me I have three years to live if I don't start taking AZT.

Six-month love affair with a rosy-cheeked boy
whose brother was dying of AIDS.
He did not believe in taking medicines
because he was against animal testing;
he was like a Christian Scientist without God.
If there was a drug that could save your brother's life,
I asked him, wouldn't you want him to take it?
He said it was an unfair question.

Standing Before the Ark

I am becoming what I will be
said the voice in the bush that burned but was not consumed.

What is ever truly without a breath of foreshadow?
What do we not seek even as we flee?

You know the consequences, your head on the block,
you cum buckets over that executioner's blade.

Do you want this scarlet letter, pink triangle?
To become what you will be?

This tag in my blood a kind of invitation, proposal, corsage.
Marked, branded, known associate—believed.

This, at least, is not a phase, not shy, awkward, a late bloomer.
This is down on my knees, I pray to the God of Sodomites.

Infection triumphant, like dying for my country, the Shema on my lips—
Hear, Oh Israel, I suck dick, I get fucked!

At the Phlebotomist's

Arm unfolds like a rose petal.
On command I make a fist, hold it
like a little boy facing off
against the schoolyard bully
(holding back hot tears—
ain't affeared o' nuthin').
He makes small talk,
passes the time while he presses
two strong fingers against the crook,
feeling for the vein.
No problem, he says;
that's what I like to hear.
Sometimes I turn my head,
avert my eyes, think...
Christmas shopping...
Labor Day cookout...
Butterfly flaps, blood flows,
one vial, another, another,
he snaps them onto the needle,
plastic tube leading
from my polluted veins.
They fill so fast,
a test-tube bouquet
bursting into crimson bloom.
What if he keeps going,
emptying my veins while the room
fills with roses?
My hand tingles.
Will   he   catch   me   when   I   swoon?
He snaps off the tourniquet,
pulls out the needle,
slaps on a Band-Aid,
and I'm free—
heading for the door
rolling down my sleeve.

Drug and Disease Free Seeks Same for Safe, Sane Sex

It began in 1990 when she was 35. They found a program in Italy that did sperm washing. She would take drugs in New York to stimulate egg production. When she was ready they would fly to Italy. He would produce a semen sample at a medical center in Milan that washed the sperm. But they did not do in vitro fertilization, which she needed because her fallopian tubes were blocked. So she would go to a center in Bologna. He would meet her there by train, a two-and-a-half-hour ride, with his washed sperm in a vacuum flask. They did this many, many times. Finally, they received a fax saying the program was being shut down; they could no longer help them. In the first week of 1997 he died of liver disease. She had a small quantity of his semen saved. A doctor in New York helped her. She conceived on the second try. Her son was born on June 6, 1999. Neither mother nor baby is infected. She may do it again. She has a little sperm left.

What the Falconer Sees

The Falconer, a bronze statue on a granite pedestal by
George Blackall Simonds, was erected in 1875 on a
prominent rock near West 72nd Street.
    —*Michele H. Bogart,*
        Public Sculpture and the Civic Ideal in
        New York City, 1890–1930

Past the powerful bird poised for flight on my wrist,
a mild winter day in Central Park—

Of the view from atop this terraced drive,
much has stayed the same in the century I've stood:

Pedestrians still mistake me for Robin Hood
in my medieval tunic and my feathered cap.

and the seasons, they come and they go—

The dry eyes of the weeping willow
will soon pour forth their tears again,
crying for joy at the coming of spring.
Or are they only green with envy
at the yellow ribbons in the forsythia's hair?

and the men, boys, they come and they go—

now worsted slacks, now jeans
Brylcreem and tie clip to ponytail and earrings
and around the time the Shah fell
purple lesions, thinning hair

And there, just now, oh—
cum drips from your ass cuz you just got fucked in the Ramble.

Who's Counting

It's all over
or it's never over
but in any case
they're gone now
with minimal
documentation
left behind
to prove
whether or not
they ever existed
and from memory
facts dissipate
and only feelings are left
like the salt
that precipitates
out of solution
when acid meets base
and water washes over
washes away
what happened.

A Poem About Dead Lovers

Only ever what I need
at any given time,
as if to take a jewel
and put it in a box,
as if to take a stone
and polish it and put it on a shelf.
You, your face in my hands,
bones of your cheek and jaw
between my fingers.

Shoe box of a studio apartment,
all the space in the world
between love and love,
the slats of the boardwalk,
between the hem of your shorts and the hair of your thighs,
your skin, all the space between the night and the stars,
between toast and French fries.

That night on the boardwalk, Cyndi in my ears—
Until it ends, there is no end.
Sometimes when I'm drunk
I understand a song lyric I could never make out before.
Like breathing, second nature, nature.

The problem is I needed to be a drummer.
The problem is I needed to play piano.
The problem is I needed a rhythm guitar.
Until Randy. Until Tony. Until Marcos.

Other Boys

Body Language

I couldn't stay hard for you,
no matter how many times we tried

to make you a boy or me a girl,
your hole into my hole,

you what I wanted.
Why did we keep at it?

Good that you were soft and milky,
but I wanted you lean and lanky,

faintly stubbled, and you wanted me to be
more of a man, the kind of man

only a woman could be.

Dream

I had a dream in which you became pregnant. We were staying in a house where the rules were very strict. I loved you and yet you had conceived that child with someone else—a boy you had snuck into your room on Christmas Eve. I snuck a boy into my room, too, but we were spotted before anything could happen, then he got nervous, and I could not convince him to stay. Some of the household were in favor of your keeping the baby, others were not. There was a meeting, like an inquest or an inquisition. My notes were confiscated, in which I had written that earlier that day, I got brave and took the dog to the forbidden island, where there was a dense downtown, tall buildings, retail establishments—you would not want to call them shopping malls—it was more elegant than that, marble floors and lofty vitrines—people who could afford to buy. When the meeting was over, Mr. Giles went out to buy us all greeting cards, so we could express our best wishes to you for your well-being and the health of the baby. The father was scared, but we tried to convince him that everything would be okay—we would help him. I wished I had that kind of support: Nobody seemed to think a great decision hung over my head; I was simply mischievous.

Other Men's Sons

Tiny brash music of the alarm clock at seven.
I wipe saliva from your lips, say I love you,

feel my own heart beating when you
lay your head on my chest,

smell your crevices, taste salt on the
soft white expanse of your throat.

Between rumpled sheets overdue for changing,
remember yesterday's sadness?

Fading, gossamer, less real
than the small raised scar that I love to touch

at the top of your soft white cheek
where he beat you.

Strike F!

In high school we sat in typing class
at neat rows of manual typewriters
with our fingers on the prescribed keys
our backs erect feet flat on the floor
while the typing teacher walked up
and down the aisles and shrilly intoned
"Strike F!" Reminiscent of how
in middle school we sat in English class
in neat rows bent over our English text
(*Adventure Book for Readers*)
while the English teacher (whose name
I remember but tactfully withhold)
walked up and down the aisles,
clutching the book to her bosom,
and shrilly intoned *the day is done*
and the darkness falls from the wings of night
as a feather is wafted downward
from an eagle in his flight like fingernails
on a blackboard those feathers wafted,
like a roomful of thirty pimply teenagers
striking F simultaneously on row
upon row of manual typewriters
while the sun shone outside
and blood stained our panties
and against the fly of our jeans
strained our cocks, their full length and girth
still something of a proud, shameful mystery.

Casual, Anonymous

Before you say a word, I am yours.
Take without asking.
Don't explore, don't discover.
Make use; make me do it.
It's all too much and not enough.
This way is better by far.

How adept we are at finding
one another—you who take
so eagerly what I so easily give;
I who swallow you whole
and taste nothing.

I perform well and you show
your appreciation just enough—
some kindness,
a deft hint at tenderness,
but still within the bounds.

Postmodernism

A mild winter day in Central Park,
when winter has begun to turn to spring
and squirrels scramble up the willow bark,
while from the ancient hurdy-gurdy ring
old melodies. The carousel spins round,
we two walk round the winding Terrace Drive
and neither of us speaks—we're Ramble bound:
There's nothing to discuss till we arrive.
My goal? To get inside his shapely ass
and make this perfect little cherub mine,
transcending bounds of gender, race, and class.
I have no lube—saliva works just fine—
and once we're through, we go our separate ways
(I lose him in the Ramble's tangled maze).

Verses for Submission

Arms pinned above my head,
powerless over what follows,

I relax my muscles,
let go the need to shape.

Legs forced aside,
events follow an order

not labored or exquisite
but natural—

microtonal polyrhythmic bluesy.

Nothing I could have invented;
so beautiful it makes me sob.

But you'd punish me if I called you a poet.

Love Poem

Bloodless death,
death without breaking the skin,
intact, clean, free from impurity,
no blood guilt to cleanse from your hands,
no avenging furies to drive you mad,
no plague on the people,
defeat in war, offense to the gods—
that's what the ancient Athenians practiced, but only
on each other: the blood of a fellow citizen
was pollution,
but the blood of a foreigner
made glisten with glory
the hoplite on whose face and hands
the gore was spattered; on his return
from battle
the city, prosperous and secure,
turned out to honor him
as I honor you, the miracle
of your bloodless surgery,
tearing my heart from my ribs,
my lungs from my chest,
cleanly, neatly,
draining me, wringing me,
leaving no trace
as you leave our field of battle
and return to your native city
a hero.

Love in the Age of Magnetic Resonance Imaging

When I saw that goon approach you,
my amygdala caught fire,
I was so afraid he'd hurt you,
I might never touch you again.
Later, when I saw you
standing on the balcony,
my ventromedial cortex
lit up like a Christmas tree—
all the good times we'd shared,
shopping, skating, the picnic
in Sheep Meadow. Then
those other girls walked by,
the ones who caught me in the kitchen
when I first arrived, pushed the hair
off my forehead and said
what a nice smile I had.
And cool waves went coursing
through my dorsolateral cortex
as I wondered if I wouldn't be
better off with one of them.

Beat Master Mike

The graffiti in the lobby reads Beat Master Mike,
        probably written by a delivery boy

or a friend of the skater kid on 17.
        But it's chilling, my name like that

inscribed on the wall, and exhilarating,
        like going under the boardwalk late at night.

I read it first as a violent exhortation—
        beat an imperative, *master* derisive,

either diminutive or ironic, but either way
        it means Who-the-fuck-do-I-think-I-am?

Then I realize it's probably a hip-hop thing,
        Beat Master, a DJ tag, and I see myself
        with two turntables and the *Iliad,*

menin aeida thea, m- m- m- menin aeida thea...

and then the tag explodes like a can of snakes—
        beat is masturbatory, or better yet, coital,
        from behind, my hands on your hips,

menin aeida thea, m- m- m- menin aeida thea...

and at first I AM THE BEAT MASTER,
        but then the Beat Master is a lean lanky

shirtless DJ with Chinese characters
        tattooed on both arms, dragons

on his chest and back,
        and we are together, but only if it's cool with him—

He could kill me as soon as fuck me,
and for all I know, he will.

The Beach at East Orleans

Flies visit, they buzz around my sandals,
sun climbs down behind my back,
rabbits forage in beach roses,
but I wait and wait, while the shadows
lengthen and the breakers pound the shore.

There are places I still feel you
pounding a rhythm inside me.
A man is sleeping in the house.
We wrap our shame around us,
smile for the camera, mug, or get taken by surprise.

There are many ends of the world;
this one ends in sand.

Fall 1981

That night Steve and I sat on a bench on West 5th Street
along the edge of Sea Breeze Park
and polished off the last six-pack
and we said good night and he went home
and I started walking down Surf Avenue
past Brightwater Towers,
carrying a brown paper bag full of empties
and the phone in the booth was ringing
and I picked it up and this guy said
I wanna lick your balls
which I thought was funny because
it seemed like he should have said
I want to suck your cock or something like that,
licking my balls seemed so half-assed,
but who was I to argue with his predilections,
whoever he was, and anyway I was so addicted
to answering phones like this I didn't hang up
although I don't remember what I said
or how our conversation went
but he told me he was under the boardwalk
just past the handball courts on West 5th Street
so I went back and I found him there
and it was the first time I'd ever gone
under the boardwalk like this
and he was a big guy, I mean heavyset,
and he was wearing a parka
which was kind of weird because it wasn't cold
and a knitted cap,
and his pants were down around his ankles
and he was jerking off and it was dark under there
and I was a little bit afraid, but more excited,
like I'd been waiting for this all along,
so I laid the bag of empties on the cold sand
and kneeled in front of him and took it in my mouth,
and I didn't care if it was clean or dirty
I just really wanted his dick in my mouth
and while I was sucking him he asked me

to put my finger in his ass, and I did,
it was disgusting but I did it anyway,
I just wanted to do as much as I could, who knew
when I would get a chance like this again
and then he asked me to fuck him,
and I was anxious about this
because I'd never done it before
and more than that it was a big thing, a big step I mean,
a kind of no-going-back, and anyway I wasn't sure
I could get hard enough, because I had trouble
getting hard enough when I was anxious,
and I was anxious right now, what with it being
under the boardwalk, late at night
with a stranger who cruised me on the fucking
pay phone for chrissake, but I wanted to
fuck him, on some level, I mean, not him exactly,
but I wanted to fuck someone,
to know, finally, what that was like,
so I went behind him, and I wasn't totally hard
really, but somehow I managed to get inside,
and it was like I was separate from myself,
I pumped, but I didn't really feel anything,
like I was fucking him with someone else's dick,
and I don't remember if I came or not
but he howled when he came
and it was hideous but also funny
and I pulled out fast and zipped up and he
pulled up his pants and I wondered what to do next,
now that I was starting to feel dirty and wrong
so I tried making some small talk,
I asked him his name, which was John of all things,
and I asked him if he did this a lot, by which I meant
get fucked under the boardwalk, and he said
Yeah, well, you know, there are some numbers you try,
by which I guess he meant numbers to pay phones,
which didn't really answer my question,
but I didn't pursue it, I just said, *Well, take care,*

and went back out into the street,
the pink glow of the sodium lamps
and cars parked along the curb
and the sidewalk deserted, and I headed back
across West 5th Street and up Surf Avenue,
my gaze fixed on that phone booth
like it was the revolver on the coffee table
and at some point I realized I had left my bag of empties
lying in the sand under the boardwalk
and I thought shit, I didn't mean to litter
and then I thought how absurd that was
under the circumstances, when I'd just fucked a man
under the boardwalk, and when I got home
I went right to the bathroom and washed my dick
with soap and water in the sink, and I wrapped it
in tissue paper for some reason before popping it
back in my underwear and zipping up my pants,
and Mom was living in Florida by then
with her boyfriend and the backyard swimming pool
and Pick 'n Pay and Winn-Dixie and
Jaxson's Ice Cream Parlour on South Federal Highway
so now it was just me and the dog and the plants
on the windowsill of our fifth-floor apartment in a state-subsidized
middle-income co-op on Surf Avenue across the street
from the police station and the firehouse and down the street
from the Bonomo factory where they made Turkish Taffy,
and I thought this living situation was fine
since I was 20 years old, a sophomore in college,
but when I'd had Thanksgiving dinner with my roommate's
family the previous November, his mother said
she thought it was criminal that my mother
had left me home alone like that,
but anyway, after I washed my dick,
I went into the living room and put on my headphones
and put Frank Sinatra on the stereo,
disc one of the *Trilogy* album, where he sings
old standards to new Billy May arrangements
and it fucking KICKS ASS, and I lay
on the living room carpet and the dog came over
and sniffed my crotch, and I thought my God, he knows,
and I blared Frank Sinatra into my headphones.

ACKNOWLEDGMENTS

These poems originally appeared, sometimes in different versions or with different titles, in the following publications.

American Poetry Review: "Postmodernism"
Assaracus: "At the Phlebotomist's," "Casual, Anonymous," "I Married a Slob,"
"Love Poem," "The Beach at East Orleans"
Brooklyn Review Online: "What the Falconer Sees"
Columbia Poetry Review: "A Poem about Dead Lovers"
Lambda Literary Review, 2015 : "Body Language"
OCHO : "Fall, 1981"
Painted Bride Quarterly: "Beat Master Mike," "Progressive Multifocal
Leukoencephalopathy"
Softblow: "The Rock"

The author acknowledges the following anthologies in which these poems appeared, sometimes in different versions or with different titles:

Divining Divas: 50 Gay Men on Their Muses. (Lethe Press, 2012), Ed. Michael
Montlack: "Progressive Multifocal Leukoencephalopathy"
Gents, Bad Boys and Barbarians: The New Gay Male Poetry, Volume Two
(Windstorm Creative, 2004), Ed. RudyKikel: "October 18, 1990,"
"Other Men's Sons," "What the Falconer Sees," "Standing before the Ark,"
"Dealing"

Thanks to Lisa Andrews and Debora Lidov for inspiring the Indolent endeavor over coffee and avocado toast in the afternoon and martinis and oysters in the evening. Your friendship and input on these poems has been invaluable. Thanks to the other poets and writers who entrusted me with their precious creative cargo: Robert Carr, Joseph Osmundson, and Sarah Sarai. Thanks to the artists who sheltered our words within the covers of their beautiful images: Justin Alves, Nayland Blake, Katie Commodore, and WT McRae. Thanks to kd diamond for creative direction, production management, and keeping me sane. Thanks to Jennie Gruber for welcoming us into her home with grace and élan. Thanks to Jason Schneiderman for his love, support, and pride. Thanks to Jameson Fitzpatrick for heeding the call to save me from myself.

ABOUT THE AUTHOR

Michael Broder is the author of *This Life Now* (A Midsummer Night's Press, 2014), a finalist for the 2015 Lambda Literary Award for Gay Poetry. His poems have appeared in *American Poetry Review, Assaracus, BLOOM, Columbia Poetry Review, Court Green, OCHO, Painted Bride Quarterly,* and other journals, as well as in the anthologies *This New Breed: Gents, Bad Boys and Barbarians 2* (Windstorm Creative, 2004), edited by Rudy Kikel; *My Diva: 65 Gay Men on the Women Who Inspire Them* (Terrace Books, 2009), edited by Michael Montlack; *Spaces Between Us: Poetry, Prose and Art on HIV/AIDS* (Third World Press, 2010), edited by Kelly Norman Ellis and ML Hunter; *Divining Divas: 50 Gay Men on Their Muses* (Lethe Press, 2012), edited by Michael Montlack; and *Multilingual Anthology: The Americas Poetry Festival of New York 2015* (Artepoética Press, 2015), edited by Carlos Aguasaco and Yrene Santos. He lives in Brooklyn with his husband, the poet Jason Schneiderman, and a backyard colony of stray and feral cats.

ABOUT INDOLENT BOOKS

Indolent Books is a small independent press founded in 2015 and operating in Brooklyn. Indolent was founded as a home for poets of a certain age who have done the creative work but for whatever reason (family, career, self-effacement, etc.) have not published a first collection. But we are not dogmatic about that mission: Ultimately, we publish books we like and care about, short or long, poetry or prose. We are queer owned, queer staffed, and maintain a commitment to diversity among our authors, artists, designers, developers, and other team members.

CPSIA information can be obtained
at www.ICGtesting.com
Printed in the USA
FFOW04n2128240117
31705FF